THE MUSIC OF EXILE

Poems by
Matthew Brennan

CLOVERDALE BOOKS

THE MUSIC OF EXILE

Poems

by Matthew Brennan

Cloverdale Books is the poetry imprint of
Wyndham Hall Press.

Library of Congress Catalog Card Number

94-061882

International Standard Book Number

1-55605-250-2

Copyright © 1994 by Matthew Brennan

ALL RIGHTS RESERVED

Printed in the United States of America

Wyndham Hall Press
Bristol, IN 46507-9460

With the support of the
Indiana Arts Commission and
National Endowment for the Arts.

ACKNOWLEDGEMENTS

Ball State University Forum: "Snowblind"

Bellingham Review: "Absence of Light"

Cape Rock: "Climax"; "Waiting at a Truck Stop in Iowa at Midnight"; "Winter Scene, Past Midnight"

Cloverdale Review of Criticism and Poetry: "Driving Home for Christmas"

Context South: "Clear Winter Nights"

Davidson Miscellany: "To the Lighthouse"

The Flying Island: "Sunset, Kensington Gardens, During the Drought"

Footwork, Paterson Literary Review: "Capture the Flag"

The Grinnell Review: "Nightshift in Central Florida"

Journal of Kentucky Studies: "Shiftwork, in February, at Terre Haute Coke and Carbon"

Kansas Quarterly: "Seeing in the Dark"; "The Gravity of Love"; "Stone Mountain"; "Autumn Landscape"

Kentucky Poetry Review: "A Splinter and a Flame"

Louisville Review: "Forward"

Mildred: "November Dusk"; "A Ghost"

Mississippi Valley Review: "Jogging at Midnight"; "The Wolf"

New Mexico Humanities Review: "Resurrection"; "Sunday Morning, in January"; *"The Adoration* and the Nativity of My Son"; "Looking for Signs"

Northern Lit Quarterly: "Fête Champêtre: The Engagement"

Passages North: "Nights Our House Comes to Life"; "The Music of Exile"

Phoebe: "A Woman Fishing"; "The Three-Bagger"

Poet Lore: "Souvenir of St. Louis"; "In the Midnight Darkness"

Sou'Wester: "End of Autumn: Lake of the Isles"

Tampa Bay Review: "Driving Home Alone, Before Twilight, on Highway 41"

Webster Review: "In Memory of My Grandfather"; "Waters Have Held Us"

Wind: "When You Don't Come Home"; "August Morning in Bloom's Bay"

Anthology of Magazine Verse and Yearbook of American Poetry: "In Memory of My Grandfather"; "Seeing in the Dark"; "Nights Our House Comes to Life"

Arts Indiana Literary Supplement, 1991: "Driving Home Alone, Before Twilight, on Highway 41"

Passages North Anthology: "Nights Our House Comes to Life"

The publication of this book is supported by grants from the Indiana Arts Commission and the National Endowment for the Arts, as well as the Arts Endowment Committee of Indiana State U.

For Beverley

TABLE OF CONTENTS

PART 1

The Music of Exile	1
Snowblind	2
The Wolf	3
Souvenir of St. Louis	4
Nights Our House Comes to Life	5
Jogging at Midnight	6
August Morning in Bloom's Bay	7
Nightshift in Central Florida	8
Climax	9
Waiting at a Truck Stop in Iowa at Midnight	10
Fête Champêtre: The Engagement	11
Preheating	12
Winter Scene, Past Midnight	13
The Adoration and the Nativity of My Son	14
A Splinter and a Flame	15
The Three-Bagger	16

PART 2

Autumn Landscape	19
Absence of Light	20
When You Don't Come Home	21
Downriver From Rouen	22
The Gravity of Love	23
A Ghost	24
Driving Home Alone, Before Twilight, on Highway 41	25
Heat Loss	26
A Singular Man in Keewanaw Bay, Michigan	27
Clear Winter Nights	28
Looking for Signs	29
Sunset, Kensington Gardens, During the Drought	30
Shiftwork, in February, at Terre Coke and Carbon	31

Driving Home for Christmas 32
Sunday Morning, in January 33
A Woman Fishing 34
Stone Mountain 35
Waters Have Held Us 36
In Memory of My Grandfather,
   William A. Brennan 37
To the Lighthouse 38
November Dusk 39
End of Autumn: Lake of the Isles 40

PART 3

Forward 43
Resurrection 44
In the Midnight Darkness 45
Air 46
The Beginning: Cancun 47
Capture the Flag 48
Seeing in the Dark 51
About the Author 52

PART

I

THE MUSIC OF EXILE

A Rachmaninoff "Prelude" penetrates
The walls from the next apartment, and suddenly my mind
Opens like ground split by an earthquake
So once again I see, if not quite feel,
What life then was really like
When, one Saturday in August, in 1959,
I barged into the kitchen
Where a piano played on the radio
And beneath the single fluorescent light
My parents--Dad sweating from yard work,
Mom aproned for cooking--abruptly
Embraced, and I stood there, embarrassed
But fiercely happy, not yet aware
That the winter night when Moscow fell
Rachmaninoff fled Russia, forever.

SNOWBLIND (For Tim)

Today, the last day of winter,
While dust is struggling like grease in water
And you're returning to your place of birth,
The mercury sinks below thirty degrees.

Driving east on 40 through mid-Missouri
You remember that cold night you first left home,
Unhurt but boiling after fighting your father;
You hardly notice that clouds, eyes swollen shut,

Are looming over the quiet fields.
Determined, you drive on into darkness
Extinguishing winter's final light
When a vortex of snow suddenly
                        descends
To the right in the ditch
Engulfing hulks in glacial ash,
To the left dimming
Headlights like mourners' eyes,

And ahead where a thin line,
An umbilical cord, leads
Your hood, inch by inch, into
The white horizon of your past.

THE WOLF

Late in the night, long after the moon set,
When air got bone-cold and deep dreams began,
We'd suddenly be wakened by great groans
Thundering through white plaster walls, bolting
From the snot clotted in my father's throat
That made his drunk snoring sound like wolf-howls
Heaved from a trap in the Wyoming rocks.

Once, in a dream, through my window I heard
Growls of a wolf at prey, and woke so choked
With fear, though I screamed with all my might,
No noise came out, just air.

                      Eight years later,
My father had cancer but no one knew;
He'd moan in his sleep, shaking the whole house
With each wild eruption of breath, till pain
Broke out in one long penetrating roar--
But I have never budged, not then, not now;
Late at night I always keep my distance:
The wolf is inside him.

SOUVENIR OF ST. LOUIS

At ten, for the first time, I left native ground:
above the Mississippi in a Pullman car,
I saw bluff-tops flush with dawn light
like new flesh molting the scab of a wound.
On the way home, we traveled at night,
trapped in a car whose air conditioner broke.
Through windows permanently shut, tar-black landscape
rolled unrelieved, and above it, wilting like corn,
burned the moon.

               Suddenly,
my father, shirt steamed to his back, stood
up, cursing full force, and herded us
into the next car where we tried to sleep;
unnerved, I couldn't, and soon opened my eyes:
beyond the coal fields of southern Illinois,
above the skyline glimmering in inky waters,
loomed the red flare of the St. Louis Arch
pumping, like an open heart, in the middle of the night.

NIGHTS OUR HOUSE COMES TO LIFE

Some nights in midwinter when the creek clogs
With ice and the spines of fir trees stiffen
Under a blank, frozen sky,
On these nights our house comes to life.
It happens when you're half asleep:
A sudden crack, a fractured dream, you bolting
upright--but all you can hear is the clock
Your great-grandfather found in 1880
And smuggled here from Dublin for his future bride,
A being as unknown to him then as she is now
To you, a being as distant as the strangers
Who built this house, and died in this room
Some cold, still night, like tonight,
When all that was heard were the rhythmic clicks
Of a pendulum, and something, barely audible,
Moving on the dark landing of the attic stairs.

JOGGING AT MIDNIGHT

A clear March night, stars arrayed
   like altar candles around a full moon,
     a corpse-face not yet cold.

Another block and the golf course
   blots the scene--ahead, where the lake
     lies melting, the path

dips like the gulf of a river valley
   whose darkness, a blackened
     lung, chars the air.

On the other side, beyond the ice, it
   rises in a bluff of firs that filters
     the blue haze of TVs across the street.

Here, at the top, loping forward you
   hit the slope covered with shadows
     unrolling like oil slicks sliding

you away from streetlight and shore
   until, at the bottom, out of breath,
     you choke on the cold, a miner

trapped in a shaft watching mud-
   slide and rocks block gleams
     of stars fading from view,

wondering how he'll ever get out.

AUGUST MORNING IN BLOOM'S BAY

All that summer you'd suffered:
Afternoons, you trudged, to kill time,
Around a brown field behind the house
Where anthills sprouted like athlete's foot
Among stunted clumps of ragweed and shrubs;
Earth, each time you lunged forward, cracked
Open wider, craving for roots.

                              At night,
When twilight, at last, had smoldered,
A sky of black syrup began to drip
Down, and the cracks closed up like morning glories.
But when darkness itself moved through the heat
And crickets were singing, *a capella*,
As if human sadness clung to their notes,
Nothing foreshadowed
The luminous August morning you'd watch
Burst over the Atlantic Ocean
From the Jersey shore, where a channel juts
Inland like a woman and enfolds the light
Till everything, as far as you can see,
Shines . . .

NIGHTSHIFT IN CENTRAL FLORIDA (For Angelo DiSalvo)

At three, I'd leave the daylight world behind,
glittering like white sand at Smyrna Beach,
and inside Spantek, Inc., would lose myself

for the next ten hours. I'd unroll two-ton
coils of steel, budge them on pulleys along
greased slides that dropped below wedged slabs, which cut

the steel sheets like cheese into silk-thin mesh.
They cut the men too. Once, some guys drank "lunch"
at the Honeybucket Bar, then two old

farts lost their thumbs when frayed gloves caught on gears
that kept on turning; and another lost
a hand tattooed in Haiti for twenty bucks.

And still the green machinery roared, concussive
rhythms that rang like shuddering subway rails,
and still I kept on rocking back and forth

on the concrete floor, too tense to miss a beat
and deaf to all but an inland murmur,
the calm vibration of a seagull's longing,

knowing come two I'd cross the empty tracks
on Miracle Mile, then take the dark road home,
a one-lane straightaway where stars spring up

like first words in a song.

CLIMAX

It is May, mid-morning; sky, sun-soaked,
glints like quartz on a Mediterranean beach;
only the east is scarred by clouds.

I am hurtling down Highway 63,
watching the lush green and black turf of Iowa farms
burst into spring right before my eyes--

all the while surfing in the wake of your warmth
utterly unaware
that I'll never be this happy again.

WAITING AT A TRUCK STOP IN IOWA AT MIDNIGHT

Daylight lingers in the orange haze
hanging like cobwebs around the horizon of trees

when, crawling behind a John Deere tractor,
you see the truck stop where you'd agreed to meet.

Here, amid nightmarish, wrinkled faces
looming bloodless in fluorescent glare,

you keep ordering coffee to pass the time;
finally, an exposed nerve, you go outside.

At this hour, when the murmurs of crickets quicken
and the cascade of traffic fades into the distance,

at this time darkness steeps in the air
and everything changes:

bleeding neon against the blackness
the truck stop casts like a lighthouse

for anything interrupting
the vastness of night,

and you, under a half-dark moon,
stand there, waiting, afraid,

as when, in the pitch dark of your bedroom,
in the dead of night, you think

you hear the floorboards creaking
and the light of morning seems

a lifetime away.

FÊTE CHAMPÊTRE: The Engagement

If only we'd known that the day Manet
Began to paint *Le Déjeuner sur l'herbe*--
An idyll of soft light, breeze, and shaded grass--
The wind hadn't breathed for nearly two weeks,
And the Seine reeked worse than a dung-clogged sewer;
If only we'd known, as we drove through back roads
By Iowa farms, watching glare make
Fenceposts sweat and blacktop blister like peasants' feet,
Then we would have kept the romance in the car--
Your grandmother's quilt, a liter of Bordeaux,
A quart of chilled water, Brie and French bread--
For beyond the barbed wire, a scene of the real:
Tar-black turf sprouting random mounds of brush,
The landscape of the long-married, who know,
As Manet knew, that fields like this are studios,
Messy, fertile beds where art ends, and life begins.

PREHEATING (For Bev)

Midsummer, heat lingers like flannel in the dusk,
beading martini glasses with sweat. We touch
our drinks together, lightly, so they clink
like strangers at an airport grazing suitcases.

We forget the gas grill preheating on the porch,
new potatoes and green beans on the stove;
all we know is desire, all we feel is the warmth
waiting in the other's grasp. There is no tomorrow,

just now. Upstairs, like passengers, we don't look down
on what we left below, coals glowing within the dark
like distant cities; nor to what awaits us--missed
connections, ruined dinners. No, instead we fly

into a banquet of flesh, blackening our bodies
on the grills of each other's bones, like Cajun fillets
cooked fast on high heat, but eaten slow.

WINTER SCENE, PAST MIDNIGHT

Past midnight, long after lovemaking,
The light patter of snow,
Like the voice of a dead child or parent,
Taps at the panes and gently wakes you.
You go to the window that opens
Out to the oak park and, beyond,
To the Art Institute's portico--
Through frost you see no moon, just clouds
Arched low like a blown-glass bowl.

You lift the window, lean into the cold,
And try to remember what you were dreaming
When, moments ago, you shuddered and woke,
Drawn for some reason into this scene.
But it's like trying to recall the instant
Your life was conceived. All you can see
Is snow falling on the still, white park,
Falling on the sculpted bronze flesh
Of some forgotten, nameless city father
Until even this solitary shape
Is nothing but white.

THE ADORATION AND THE NATIVITY OF MY SON (For Dan)

Death is what we fear most
but birth, only, can hold the world:
as in Leonardo, you'll see someday,
beyond a small arc of family and friends,
and the perfect lines of picturesque
ruins, life seems an unrelieved blur
of every possible motive and angle
clashing like wild hysterical horses,
or left unpainted, like these mountains,
to dissolve like dust in the distance.

It's this chaos, though, that gives
you birth its unity:
the circle of adorers, like half-
formed intuitions, surround
Madonna and child and flow
around them like dawn light;
but notice, too, in the corner,
a youth deserting the old order--
a pillar of your solid foreground--

has already turned away
to see what else the light is on.

A SPLINTER AND A FLAME

When a child is sick--
Your only begotten son,
His flesh a furnace kicking in
During a February blizzard--
Then, in the warm irregular puffs
Of the little boy's breathing, you feel
What luck it takes just to be born,
The single beached splinter of the nightly
Sinking of a thousand wrecked ships.
But you feel luckier still to have borne
This small-boned, delicate child this long,
To have kept him burning at all,
Like a wooden-match flame in a hurricane.

THE THREE-BAGGER

Like clockwork, when the crickets began to chitter
And winds vacuumed the malt of humidity from the air,
My grandfather'd cart a stool from the kitchen
To the dark corner where the radio still squats.
He'd crouch low, cupping his deaf ear as if it hurt,
And would strain, in a trance, to hear
The perpendicular thwack
Of swung wood and hurled rawhide connecting . . .

Just once, on a sandlot, before his twelfth birthday,
He cracked a corkball with a broomhandle so far
He forgot to run at first, it felt so good,
And still made a three-bagger, standing up.
The oldest of eight, he was drafted to fix
Sockets and wire lights before he saw his first curve
And so could only listen, while his brothers
Broke in with clubs in the 3-I League,
And one of them, one summer, made it with Cleveland.

I imagine him still listening, even now,
Crouched upstairs above the vent in the wall:
On the mound in the basement with the count
Full, I lob the dog's ball, underhand,
To "Willie McGee," my four-year-old boy:
He becomes a transparent eyeball blending
His swing with the pitch--and as long
As the sound lasts--connecting us all.

PART

II

AUTUMN LANDSCAPE

The landscape, this morning, is suddenly changed:
Red leaves are falling, wheeling from treetops
Like bloodied kestrels carried away
By dreams of a southerly breeze.
                            And in the east
White light blazes, briefly, then smolders
In cold clouds, like an old priest, heartsick,
Hungering for the feel of his young neighbor's wife.

And in the west, where darkness is sleeping in,
Frost gnaws on pine needles and deadwood
From two trees that, last spring, glowed green,
Still luminous, like the eyes of a child
Who believes that love will never end
And that the life of his growing body
Is something that could never die.

ABSENCE OF LIGHT

Last night we fought: you said the stress of marriage,
of modern life as we live it, is so
great these days you feel you're pinned to the ropes
by a championship wrestler who throws
his gross bulk around like Dick the Bruiser
or some Masked Marvel; air, like rope, grew taut,
and you said maybe I should move downtown,
get a room with one chair, one light, one cot.

Suddenly, I could see ten years from now,
could see snow fall across Iowa farms
through a Greyhound window, could see the dark
of a cold winter night expunge the charms
of another strange town, where, past midnight
in a bar, my eyes are framed by absence of light.

WHEN YOU DON'T COME HOME

When you look his way
Day grows blacker than the cassock of a priest
Swinging incense

When you pronounce his name
Air smells darker than the black fur between your thighs
While they press together like fingertips, barely
Touching, in church

And when you don't come home
I am the child in the red shirt,
Locked out of the house,
And helplessly watching black clouds drop
Like bulls trampling the heart of Barcelona.

DOWNRIVER FROM ROUEN

A barge merges, downriver from Rouen,
With white fog; it trudges upstream around
A bend like a tired fat man treading water;
And then, curving left, it lets the pilot
Catch the edge of stone roads where villas,
Here and there, relieve the gray, moonless sky
With the glitter of distant bedroom windows.

One window, ahead, shines through clasped shutters
Of a second-story study. But the pilot is blind
To stacked books, coffee cups, and paper;
He pictures his wife's white thighs visible, barely,
Beneath thin, white cloth. He can't see what,
Through the black slats, the lamp lights up:
A sweaty writer carving phrases in vellum
Who has just read the pilot's mind and pictures
A pretty but aging woman, bored with life and sick
With the "exquisite sweetness" of romanticism.

Later, the fog clears like the mind at daybreak,
Flaubert gets in bed, and, five miles away,
The pilot guides his barge toward the moon,
Which lounges, quartered, around the next bend.

THE GRAVITY OF LOVE

Ten years ago, at Heathrow Airport, our bodies
Touched, like the orbits of two planets coming
Together at last, guided since creation
By the gravity of love. Now we're apart.
You have your own space. But still, at night,
Above the dark that hides the dead trees,
And the scarred fields upturned like graves,
The same stars shine
                          light-years away.

A GHOST

The fall of the quake my marriage died:
It had rained for days; the sodden green lawns
Looked lush as poured paint, and mist dripped
Constantly, clinging to black bark and wood walls
Like cobwebs covering a boarded window.

And now, on Halloween night,
Even after the earth has closed
And new gardens have forced their first yields,
Something rotten stirs underground,
A ghost squirming in a suicide's grave,

And though I've redrawn with fresh paint
The landscape of my life,
Like a surreal pentimento
                              her face--
In a beautifully grotesque Cubist pose--
Still shows through, fragmented and jagged.

DRIVING HOME ALONE, BEFORE TWILIGHT, ON HIGHWAY 41
(For Richard)

The slant of light on August corn,
twenty miles from Terre Haute, slides
a long-hidden dusk inside the view
his windshield frames. Ahead, haze
hangs like blonde hair, windblown in back.
A mile more and sky, beaten
red, begins to breathe in blue streaks,
so he thinks again of her face, the way,
when flushed, it could feel the dark
coming of long, cool nights, however far off.

Five years ago, when the air wouldn't move,
they moved in, in the dark, then slept together
on a hardwood floor, splintered but washed,
he recalls, with streetlight white as sheets
or gauze. Afterwards, though, she dozed as if
closed up in a husk, while, wide-eyed, he heard
the empty boxcars and rumbling trucks
and through the high, bare windows watched
stars, like sad women starting over, drive
straight out of town, not once looking back.

HEAT LOSS

3:30 a.m., and you know the cold
woke you, not the unraveling dream of almost
coupling with some camisoled blonde. Since ten,
frost's caked the windows white, and the wool afghan's
sunk to the parquet floor. But since the spread
still hugs your form, you sense that something's wrong.
Something else is gone: the hub of your house
no longer pumps; a broken-hearted fool,
the furnace fluttered for a while, but now
its thermostat just won't turn on. The heart
has lost its warmth, and where it used to burn
blue with desire, a dark indifference grows
and flows through vents in closets, halls, and rooms
until it fills all grooves, like hardening ice--
so now, if you roll where the sheets don't drift,
you'll freeze, like a single stick in the blowing
snow, helpless to spark itself into fire.

A SINGULAR MAN IN KEEWANAW BAY, MICHIGAN

Because he thought a lot how life might end,
Sat on the dock each night and watched the sun
Dissolve in a headland of Douglas firs;

Because he stayed until the cold black waters
Grew still as first stars that come on so slowly
Nobody notices when they've been there

Since dark; and because he never felt alone
While the moon rose above the toppled bricks
Of the old Ford plant, bleaching them like stones,

When his wife left one May, just as snow fell,
He knew, at last, he'd never leave the bay,

Where, from dock's edge, a man can watch the nights begin.

CLEAR WINTER NIGHTS

Seventeen years ago, a clear winter night:
I'm walking, alone, on snow not yet shoveled
through boot prints, bike tracks, and ruts

when, suddenly, my eye meets
a window glowing like a girl whose half-slip
hangs, in mid-air, between white hips

and floorboards cold as concrete. And just
then, though too far away, the full moon
comes between black branches of a chestnut tree.

Another winter night--an entire lifetime
later, I'm retracing the same tracks
through new snow as white as the back of the moon

which still shines, exposed,
like the curve of familiar, untouched
flesh, only lower in the sky.

LOOKING FOR SIGNS

After Mom weathered the battery of CAT-scans,
we waited a week for the final news.
I looked wildly for signs everywhere:
when the plumber repaired a pipe torn
loose below the kitchen sink, I saw
a worn colon, ruptured then transformed
to an organ that glowed like ruddy copper.
And when the street crew patched potholes
at 13th and Crawford, making skin grafts
of asphalt, I saw holes closed where lumps
had been, tumors like tulip-bulbs that grew
underground. And then when the car mechanic
called to say the strange sound in the engine's
benign, I thanked him profusely, as if he meant
the life he saved had been her own, as if
I hadn't known all along I'd trade it in
at a New Year's sale, grateful for good riddance.

SUNSET, KENSINGTON GARDENS, DURING THE DROUGHT

Late July in London, but a cold breeze
blows from Scotland, storm clouds crossing
the bloodshot sky like black birds flying in front
of doubledecker buses. From my canvas chair, under plane trees
fifty feet from the walk, I've watched the light
beneath the trees turn purple as a bruise,
watched the pond's algaed waves suddenly
convulse, and footwork of passersby quicken
with coming darkness. Now near night,
the landscape quiets, waiting for prayed-for rain
like dreamless sleep. But nesting on the adjacent bench,
a Pakistani's curled up, a nightmare waiting to happen,
my cue to move on, to find a dry, lively pub.

SHIFTWORK, IN FEBRUARY, AT
TERRE HAUTE COKE AND CARBON

In winter, the cranes start eating
the mounds of black coke while it's still
dark out. On mornings so cold their numb tires
turn like blocks of ice, the smokestacks
cough up inky columns of snot and spit,
and the train tracks that vein the grounds
throb already under gauze strips of frost.
Even coal cars, empty at midnight, squat
hunchbacked with half-loads by the open docks.

Meanwhile, across the road, a small graveyard
glows in the refrigerated air; tombstones
shine like typewriter keys used to punch out
the morning obits. But now, they're as white
with untouched snow as blank newsprint waiting
for someone to make a lasting impression.

DRIVING HOME FOR CHRISTMAS

The interstate I'd seen a hundred times,
in all seasons, all angles of light, lost
its contours in gray vapor that poured
forty feet ahead and spread in all directions,

turning the landscape of woods and farms I knew
mile by mile into a land of unlikeness,
a land like the one in which my grandmother's mind
now lives, the past like photos she memorized

but misplaced, and the present, an eye
that can't shut, or a road that won't end.

SUNDAY MORNING, IN JANUARY

Through an opaque lens of glass and ice, sunlight slants
Inside, level with the lopsided double bed;
Waking, you blink at the refraction,
Stunned now as at birth eighty years ago:
A burning white light in a cold white room.
Snowblind, you slowly sense that what wakes you
Is a warmth you can't quite feel yet know is
Here, a presence that seems always about to embrace you--

But then fades, like a recurring dream never quite
Remembered, or like the worn faces of the dead,
Whose images you smudge a bit more each time
You wake and reproduce them in your mind
While the world is hardening, as it is right now,
In the light of Sunday morning, in January.

A WOMAN FISHING (For Louise Simon)

Another day is ending in northern Minnesota,
Where a widow, alone in a lifeboat, is
Drifting, far from shore, on the still waters of a deep lake.

Soon, the woman's dark form becomes a silhouette
Against the amber of the far distance
That gleams with the last light of the buried sun.

As if she waited all day for this one
Moment, when the day is dead but the long night
Is not yet born, and the ghost-like moon is not awake,

Now, for a few seconds only, she feels again
The glow of her husband, the single being
Whose life she's loved for fifty years, whose pole

She now holds like a blind woman's cane,
Casting into that cold, endless darkness.

STONE MOUNTAIN (To the Memory of Doug Johnson, Who Fell off Stone Mountain, January, 1981)

At last, from your hometown, there is no motion;
on a crag jutting into shade, your right
boot just happened to graze ice whisking
you off into the physics of falling snow.

Now, it has stopped falling; the wind,
piling drifts by graves all afternoon, blows
somewhere else; and clouds, like gauze pads,
sop the wound of the quarter-moon . . .

There was such speed in your supple body
cleaving like a bronze rudder the blue lengths of the pool,
floodlights would sparkle in your wake like sharks.
But light moves faster in air than in water:

Come morning, sun will shine on Stone Mountain
as if nothing, nothing at all, had stopped.

WATERS HAVE HELD US (In Memory of Deane Postlethwaite)

1
Kansas, March 1925

Moonlight fills half-frozen puddles
in muddy furrows which, like cupped hands,
hold stray seeds trying to take root.
Near the woods, a farmer stands in darkness,
boots entrenched in the black thaw,
and watches each evening before going to bed
for the first crow to swoop over the land,
over the house a hundred yards away
where his wife, nine-months pregnant,
already is dreaming.

2
Minnesota, October 1980

Restless clouds, like an insomniac's sheets,
scramble all day and infuse the air
with the impulse of change. You,
restless, too, with Nikon in hand,
scour the retreat grounds looking
for intermittent flashes of light.
Just before sunset, by the pond, you
catch the gleam on a gull's wing
rising to wheel it away--then, clouds
break, driving you inside,
like a seed withdrawing
into the earth.

IN MEMORY OF MY GRANDFATHER, WILLIAM A. BRENNAN (1882-1972)

I have a photograph Dad took in 1957
of Pop and me sharing an armchair and showing
the same complacent, incipient smile--
as if he knew some secret and, without a single
syllable or motion, had impressed it on my mind.

I've never remembered posing for that picture,
parting my lips to inhale the breath he just sighed--
but engraved in time like Dürer woodcuts
are the stories he'd tell in Forest Park
where afternoon light would hit his face and hold,
for an instant, the gleam that gave his eyes their look:

Like the time installing spotlights in the dark dome
of the Arena ceiling, he lost footing and fell
off the scaffold, but having, that morning, shunned
suspenders for a thick cowhide belt, he was
caught by the buckle by his partner's free hand.

Or the time he boarded the train bound for Topeka
and got off to sleep in Boonville before moving on--
but feeling sick and restless checked out
and rode all the way home, where he read the next day
the hotel had burned down, everything reduced to ashes
so no one could tell one corpse from another.

On that last Thanksgiving, my first visit in two months,
he wore the same gay smile, lying
shriveled in the bedsheets like a leprechaun:
I see myself bending for the last press of his lips--
but I never saw him again, never
asked how to charge this etching with ink.

TO THE LIGHTHOUSE (In Memory of My Grandfather, Jerome I. Simon, 1902-1980)

In your mind, right now, it must be
Bloomsbury, London, 1926:
After a long hot set at the Cora Hotel
Cooking jazz in the back ballroom
On a black Baby Grand,
You've been walking alone tonight
Under a heavy, starless sky;
It fills, suddenly,
The open window of a building
One block away
Where Virginia Woolf is lying sleepless
Wondering how her novel will end--
In your mind, right now, that instant
Before clouds burst,
Lightning streaking across dark glass,
Flaring, and giving out
In an ocean of
Gray

The gray of your final New Year's Eve,
The last time your hands fluttered
Like swans over the keys
And you lifted your face, eyes closed,

Toward the light that you alone can see.

NOVEMBER DUSK

Because last leaves have fallen, a new view
Blooms through the living room glass: the cold, gnarled
Branches of a sixty-year-old oak warm
Their worn knuckles in the glow of a light
Whose wax is gone. But the tree's freezing palms
Shine black, curved eastward like hands that have held
Death in dark, quiet rooms, hands that won't heal.
And though they'll never hold again the green
Coming of buds in early March, they'll stay
Open all winter, waving goodbye.

END OF AUTUMN: Lake of the Isles

Late afternoons by Lake of the Isles
An old man sits alone in the sand
Surrounded by a museum of debris:
Coke bottles, goose turds, twigs, and dead leaves.

Always he watches the wind love the water
Glistening in the dusk like flesh just kissed;
Always he listens for the sounds the lake makes,
Always as if straining to hear human voices.

And always, as night falls and ice starts to form,
He listens for gulls somewhere in the distance
As if come darkness they will tell him
When to rise and walk on the water.

PART

III

FORWARD

Driving north on a back road in the twilight
Of April, the warmest day since last September
When a hard frost killed my black-thumbed marriage,
I watch the sun, like a sacrifice, bleed to death
Above green farms in eastern Indiana, in fields
Where life's just returned and nothing's ripe.

But still on the same road, I'm going
North from the broken lives that lie
Behind me, where day's already
Left, like a car hurtling
Forward from the dead body of a tire,
Its driver gripping the wheel

Like a lifeline he hopes will pull
Him from dark waters and into the air
Where light, if nothing else, will soon grow back.

RESURRECTION

My job these days is to cut lumber
at the Ace Hardware store. Often, too,
I do the inventory. It's then
when the past can come back, and I
need to go home, build a small fire,
and watch the logs go up in smoke,
dead trees transformed into something else.
In Nam, my job was to bring back
the bodies on flatbed trucks, stacked
in rows like cords of wood. Sometimes,
if a mine blew up in a muddy
rice field where five men had
crouched in soupy water, blood would
flood them like a bouillabaisse--we'd
fish out what we could. But once
when a ship got bombed off harbor
in waves clear as a bathroom mirror, I went
down to count the dead, then sent them
upwards, one by one, like balloons
let go, allowed at last to rise
in the light like motes of yellow dust.

IN THE MIDNIGHT DARKNESS

The wind rolls in like the cold Pacific surf
And carries with it the muffled cry, far
Off, of a child lost in the midnight darkness.

Its voice, the dull knife of guilt, cuts
Me off--so long ago abandoned, like photos
Of the dead dumped in a basement,

The face stays hidden: It is trapped,
Sunk in muddy waters, waiting for me to learn again
How to see in the dark, how to hear under water.

AIR

After ten days of tiffs and suffocating heat,
it happened: cool westerly winds parted
the curtains like fingers fitted between
wet lips; outside, trees teetered lazily,
like a girl, eyes closed, swaying to soft
music, while above a half-dozen clouds,
egg whites in a blue bowl, floated
over the horizon, suddenly unimportant,
worries just forgotten. And then I knew
my lungs breathed in a fullness
that found room for words, for lyrics
to the broken melody she'd listened to so long--
the song we could hum to, but had not yet sung.

THE BEGINNING: Cancun (For Beverley)

Your plane swoops over jungle
Just as the sun plummets into
Lagoon water. Charcoal darkness
Rises like ruins, though it's only
Four. You're sure you are where you've
Never been, yet it feels real--
A face you know but can't place--

But then the moon bobs its head through
Tinted bus windows; you see
Her smile, brightening like hotel lights
Coming on.
        In old age, these lights
Are what you'll remember most, not
The dark.
        So, tonight, you'll sleep,
Spoon-style, dreaming of elsewhere,

Until the Caribbean Sea
Grows green as beer bottles
And tanned boys earning their breakfast
Rake the white sand clean.

CAPTURE THE FLAG (For Mike)

I

It's Christmas, 1975. We're drunk,
Standing outside in front of Tim's apartment,
The darkness swirling in the space between us
Like snow that flurries all night, never sticking
To anything. It seems blacker now than
Any night since finding you, by chance,
At Camp St. Paul, whose midnight woods could blind.
Inside, the other two exchange goodbyes,
The only end to tales of family sadness.
Meanwhile, white clouds of words snow toward me from
Your mouth: *I've always felt that we were closest
Of us four brothers*.   Stunned, I feel snowblind,
Avalanched in guilt I never saw.

II

Tonight, I just can't sleep: the noise of crickets
Sounds dark, their thin persistent buzz like wires
Shorting out in a brown yard in late August.
They're mourning the death of the god of summer.
I guess I'm mourning something too: today
You're thirty-four, and now we've spent about
Half of your life apart, almost as if
The first half never happened, or got lost
In some past we cannot see, can't remember
Like photos we forget we ever posed for--
The past of history, what I read this morning
In a used book about the Civil War
Of brothers, blue and gray, who killed each other.

III

But nights I see the moon caught in crosshairs
Of branches out my window, my deep memory
Opens like a shutter; then I remember
Darkness in our past, the nights I woke,
Alone, from a bad dream and couldn't close
My eyes for fear something was looking in.
Something dark was out there--something so vague,
So vast dreams could never picture it,
So I would go to your bed; I'd hug you,
Relieved that you were still inside but knowing
That it was there, still waiting for the rest
Of our lives, for whatever was left. But
Like light, come morning, you were always here.

And in that hard light of morning I'd face
My shadow. Darkness spread before me like
A huge black snake whose back I walked upon.
And you too, little brother, lived beneath
Me, subject to my looming ego's power:
Like the time we spent the night together
Across the street. When you left early, not
Waiting to eat the breakfast fixed for us,
I chased you down in a neighbor's yard, knocked
You flat, then drummed my fists against your ribs
Until the final sobs left your lungs. I
Went back and ate for two. But what's worse, you
Forgave me, like a blind man's loyal dog.

IV

Yes, you are always here, like morning light.
Like the night at Camp St. Paul, when we played
Capture the Flag, one half against the other.
A steady current of blurred bodies rushed
Like smoke-fringed troops past trees, while the night crept
Up, though no one knew it yet. What I knew
As their yells fell cascading forward in
Hysteria, was that I felt alone,

Homesick for a brother lost across
A line some counselor'd drawn in dirt. A line
My fear wouldn't let me break. Then, when no one
Yelled and the darkness swelled round me so all
I sensed was a pregnant calm, I saw you.

V

That moment--together for the first time
All week (our first apart)--was brief: I soon
Let you go, to save you. And as we stood
There, darkness in the distant faces, quiet
Rising with the night, I knew it was bound
To end, that darkness, not the light, would win.
But New Year's Day you wore the olive tie
I gave you this Christmas. And you wear it
Still in the picture propped against my reading
Lamp--a snapshot taken by my son
Of us two brothers, on top of the World
Trade Center, where, heads turned, we're watching late
Daylight gleam on the icy Verrazano Bridge.

SEEING IN THE DARK

Below my father's house, lies a river valley
where the Mississippi rolls, lifting mist
in the morning till sunlight consumes it,
slowly, the way dogs dally round dishes
when watched. At night, barge-warnings
echo up the bluff and die on our doorstep.
Sometimes, if the moon strikes you right,
and the cold air smells clean, the night pulls
you inward before you can stop
and, as you're swallowed, turns
you inside out--there
                      in darkness
blindness becomes sight, and you see
how the world looks to those dying,
before first dawn light, when the moon
is glowing like a darkroom lamp
and the landscape is a negative,
undeveloped, waiting for
immersion.

ABOUT THE AUTHOR

Matthew Brennan was born in St. Louis and educated at Grinnell College and the University of Minnesota, where he also served for a year as a visiting assistant professor of English. Since 1985 he has taught at Indiana State U. in Terre Haute, where he lives with his son, Dan, and the pianist Beverley Simms. He has published two other books: *Seeing in the Dark: Poems* (Hawkhead Press, 1993); and *Wordsworth, Turner, and Romantic Landscape* (Camden House, 1987). He has also contributed poems, articles, and reviews to numerous journals, including *Poet Lore, Mississippi Valley Review, Kansas Quarterly, Cloverdale Review, Georgia Review, Poetry Ireland Review, South Atlantic Quarterly, Verse,* and *New Mexico Humanities Review.*